JAMES WATSON

Other titles in the
NOBEL PRIZE-WINNING SCIENTISTS *series*:

MARIE CURIE
0-7660-2170-X

ALBERT EINSTEIN
0-7660-2185-8

ENRICO FERMI
0-7660-2177-7

GUGLIELMO MARCONI
0-7660-2280-3

LINUS PAULING
0-7660-2130-0

JAMES WATSON
0-7660-2258-7

NOBEL PRIZE-WINNING

SCIENTISTS

JAMES WATSON

SOLVING THE MYSTERY OF DNA

Janet Hamilton

Enslow Publishers, Inc.

40 Industrial Road   PO Box 38
Box 398   Aldershot
Berkeley Heights, NJ 07922   Hants GU12 6BP
USA   UK

http://www.enslow.com

> *"The discovery of [DNA] is of great importance because it outlines the possibilities for understanding [the] individual properties of living matter."*
>
> —Professor A. Engstrom

Library of Congress Cataloging-in-Publication Data

Hamilton, Janet.
    James Watson : solving the mystery of DNA / Janet Hamilton.—1st ed.
        p. cm.—(Nobel Prize-winning scientists)
    Summary: A biography of James Watson, one of the scientists who helped discover the structure of DNA, the carrier of heredity in higher organisms.
    Includes bibliographical references and index.
    ISBN 0-7660-2258-7
    1. Watson, James D., 1928—Juvenile literature. 2. Molecular biologists—United States—Biography—Juvenile literature. 3. DNA—Juvenile literature. [1. Watson, James D., 1928- 2. Molecular biologists. 3. Scientists. 4. DNA.] I. Title. II. Series.
    QH506.W4H35   2004
    572.8'092—dc22

                        2003022972

Printed in the United States of America

10 9 8 7 6 5 4 3 2 1

To Our Readers:
We have done our best to make sure all Internet Addresses in this book were active and appropriate when we went to press. However, the author and the publisher have no control over and assume no liability for the material available on those Internet sites or on other Web sites they may link to. Any comments or suggestions can be sent by e-mail to comments@enslow.com or to the address on the back cover.

Every effort has been made to locate all copyright holders of material used in this book. If any errors or omissions have occurred, corrections will be made in future editions of this book.

Illustration Credits: © The Nobel Foundation, p. 7; A. Barrington Brown/Science Photo Library, p. 69; ArtToday.com, pp. 16, 43, 86; Courtesy of the Cold Spring Harbor Laboratory, pp. 11, 20, 22, 23, 28, 33, 51, 58, 60, 61, 65, 67, 74, 76, 79, 83; David Torsiello/Enslow Publishers, Inc., pp. 55, 71; Donald Jenkins/National Library of Medicine, p. 47; Enslow Publishers, Inc., p. 41; National Library of Medicine, p. 39; Pressens Bild, p. 13.

Cover Illustration: AP/Wide World Photos (foreground); ArtToday.com (background).

CONTENTS

DEDICATION

For my parents, Anne and Bruce Dawson,
whose contributions to me go beyond genetics.

THE NOBEL PRIZE

Almost every year since its founding in 1901, the Nobel Prize has been awarded to individuals who have distinguished themselves in the fields of physiology or medicine, physics, chemistry, literature, and peace. (In 1968 a prize for economics was added.) The prize is named for Alfred Nobel, a Swede born in Stockholm in 1833, who grew up to become a successful chemist, manufacturer, and businessman.

Nobel began experimenting with ways to make nitroglycerine, an explosive, safer for practical use. Eventually he found a way to make a paste of nitroglycerine mixed with silica. He could then shape the paste into a stick that could be placed in holes drilled in rocks. He patented this creation in 1867 and named it dynamite. In order to detonate the dynamite sticks, Nobel also invented a blasting cap that could be ignited by burning a fuse. The invention of dynamite, along with equipment like the diamond drilling crown and the pneumatic drill, significantly reduced the expenses associated with many types of construction work.

Soon Nobel's dynamite and blasting caps were in great demand. Nobel proved to be an astute businessman, establishing companies and laboratories throughout the world. He also continued to experiment with other chemical inventions and held more than 350 patents in his lifetime.

Alfred Nobel did not narrow his learning to scientific knowledge alone. His love of literature and poetry prompted him to write his own works, and his social conscience kept him interested in peace-related issues.

When Nobel died on December 10, 1896, and his will was read, everyone was surprised to learn that he left instructions for the accumulated fortune from his companies and business ventures (estimated at more than $3 million U.S.) to be used to award prizes in physics, chemistry, physiology or medicine, literature, and peace.

In fulfilling Alfred Nobel's will, the Nobel Foundation was established in order to oversee the funds left by Nobel and to coordinate the work of the prize-awarding institutions. Nobel prizes are presented every December 10, the anniversary of Alfred Nobel's death.

THE SECRETS OF LIFE

"We wish to suggest a structure for the salt of deoxyribose nucleic acid (DNA). This structure has novel features which are of considerable biological interest."[1] With these words, James Watson and Francis Crick announced their discovery of the structure of DNA in 1953. Nine years later, along with Maurice Wilkins, they were awarded the Nobel Prize in Physiology or Medicine for their work.

In his presentation of the Nobel Prize, Professor A. Engstrom explained the significance of the discovery:

> The discovery of the three-dimensional molecular structure of the deoxyribonucleic acid—DNA—is of great importance because it outlines the possibilities for an understanding in its finest details of the molecular configuration, which dictates the general and individual properties of living matter. DNA is the substance which is the carrier of heredity in higher organisms.[2]

To say that American James Watson was an unlikely choice to make this discovery would be an understatement.

Originally trained to study birds, he disliked chemistry and avoided it through college and much of graduate school. Later he teamed up with Englishman Francis Crick, originally a physicist who was still in the process of getting his Ph.D. in biology when they made the DNA discovery. In his Nobel lecture Watson stated:

> [W]ith Francis to talk to, my fate was sealed. For we quickly discovered that we thought the same way about biology. The center of biology was the gene and its control of cellular metabolism. The main challenge in biology was to understand gene replication and the way in which genes control protein synthesis. It was obvious that these problems could be logically attacked only when the structure of the gene became known. This meant solving the structure of DNA. Then this objective seemed out of reach to the interested geneticists. But in our cold, dark Cavendish lab, we thought the job could be done, quite possibly within a few months.[3]

This youthful optimism (Watson was only twenty-four and Crick was thirty-six when they made their discovery) led Watson and Crick to persevere and find the correct solution. Although Maurice Wilkins was awarded the Nobel Prize along with Watson and Crick, another important contributor was not. Wilkins' colleague at King's College, Rosalind Franklin, was a scientist who had done groundbreaking work with DNA. Her photograph of the DNA molecule had led directly to the model Watson and Crick designed. Her early death, in 1958 at the age of thirty-seven, meant she could not be awarded a Nobel Prize, as the prizes are only given to living scientists. Since only three

NOBEL PRIZE WINNERS AT THE 1962 CEREMONY (FROM LEFT TO RIGHT): MAURICE WILKINS, MAX PERUTZ (FOR CHEMISTRY), FRANCIS CRICK, JOHN STEINBECK (FOR LITERATURE), JAMES WATSON, AND JOHN KENDREW (FOR CHEMISTRY).

people can share the Nobel, there will always be a question as to whether or not she would have won.

Why was the discovery of DNA structure important enough to win James Watson and his colleagues a Nobel Prize? To answer this question, it is necessary to look at exactly what DNA is and what scientists have learned about DNA since Watson, Crick, and Wilkins made their discoveries.

DNA is part of a big puzzle that scientists have been trying to solve for centuries. People have always observed that different traits are passed down from parents to their offspring. Throughout history, there have been various explanations offered for this phenomenon. By the middle of the twentieth century, scientists had learned that genes were what determined heredity, and that DNA, which contained the genes, was the key to the process. What they still did not understand was how DNA carries the genetic information and how the DNA makes a copy of itself, or replicates, during the process of cell division.

In figuring out the structure of DNA, Watson and Crick were able to answer the question of how genes replicate. This was a key discovery, but it did not allow them to see the whole picture. Since that discovery, scientists have solved most of the puzzle, but there are still pieces missing. Looking at what we know today allows us to see the importance of Watson and Crick's contribution.

Every living thing is made up of cells. In the center of each cell is the nucleus, which contains chromosomes. Chromosomes travel in pairs. When any living thing reproduces sexually, each parent contributes one half of the genetic material. One chromosome in each pair in the nucleus of the new cell is from the father and one is from the mother.

Each chromosome is made up of proteins and a long strand of DNA. How long is this strand? A cell is tinier than the tiniest dot you can see, and the DNA inside it is three feet long. This long strand is coiled so tightly that it can fit into the cell. Thanks to James Watson and Francis Crick, we now know the structure of DNA. It is in the shape of a spiral or helix. There are two strands to the helix. These strands are connected by weak chemical bonds. Each strand is made up of four bases: adenine, guanine, thymine, and cytosine. The bases always pair up in the same way. If adenine is on one strand it will always bond with thymine on the other strand. Likewise, guanine and cytosine always bond.

Genes are located along this DNA helix. About 5 percent of DNA is genes. Scientists are not sure what the rest of DNA is used for. Most genes consist of several thousand pairs of bases. The order of the pairs determines the kind of protein the cell will make. The function of the cell, such as repairing skin or building muscle, depends on the kind of protein it makes.

Cells reproduce by dividing in two. Each pair of new cells contains the original DNA. We now know that DNA is the key to cell reproduction. Before a cell divides, it reproduces its DNA. The two strands that make up the helix of

JAMES WATSON RECEIVES HIS NOBEL PRIZE FROM KING GUSTAV VI OF SWEDEN ON DECEMBER 10, 1962.

DNA split. The two individual strands are templates for forming two DNA molecules that are identical to the original. Bases from the nucleus of the cell (adenine, cytosine, guanine, and thymine) bond with the bases on each strand to form the new DNA in the two new cells.

The discovery of the structure of DNA was the beginning of a revolution in biology that continues to this day. Scientists have learned much more about genetics during the past fifty years, and their work is often in the news.

One fascinating way scientists have used DNA is to create DNA "fingerprints" that allow them to solve crimes. If police can obtain anything from a crime scene that contains a person's cells—hair, skin, saliva, etc.—they can get such a fingerprint. Once the DNA is taken from the sample, it is mixed with enzymes that break it apart. An electric current moves the fragments through a gel. Larger, heavier pieces move more slowly than smaller, lighter ones, so the sample can be sorted by length and weight. A print is made from the results. It is a pattern of bars, similar to a bar code. Each person's DNA pattern is unique.

If a suspect in a crime is caught, a new print can be made from cells obtained from the person in question. This print is compared to the one already in existence. If the prints are identical, the suspect may be the criminal. No one else, except an identical twin, could have the same DNA pattern.

Another way the science of genetics is being used is to treat people with inherited diseases. At this point, scientists are still working on locating genes that cause diseases. For example, in 1989 Dr. Lap-Chee Tsui, a scientist working at the Hospital for Sick Children in Toronto, Canada, was able to discover the gene that causes the disease cystic fibrosis. Although this gene is missing the DNA code for just one amino acid in a single protein, it causes a disease that results in death before the age of twenty-five.

While the cause of cystic fibrosis has been discovered, scientists are still working to discover a cure. Knowledge of genetics has been used, however, to treat people with other diseases. Genes can be inserted directly into white blood cells, and then injected back into the body. This treatment has been used to help people who have illnesses that make them unable to fight off any kind of infection.

Perhaps the most famous use of genetics is cloning. In February 1997, news headlines announced the birth of a sheep named Dolly, the first cloned mammal. Dolly was created by scientists who took a cell from another sheep and removed the nucleus. The nucleus was then implanted into an egg that had had its DNA removed. The fertilized egg was then stimulated to begin dividing and reproducing. Of 276 eggs that were treated this way, 29 seemed to be developing after six days. These 29 were implanted into ewes, and one resulted in Dolly's birth. Dolly had the exact same genes as the sheep from which she was cloned.

Since then, several types of mammals have been cloned. Pigs and goats were first cloned in 2000, cats and rabbits in 2002, and a horse in 2003. Cloning the first horse led to ethical questions about whether or not cloned horses would be allowed to compete in horse races. So far, the Jockey Club, the organization that controls thoroughbred racing, has outlawed it. Some scientists hope that the successful cloning of mammals may lead to saving endangered species some day.

A SHEEP WAS THE FIRST SUCCESSFULLY CLONED MAMMAL, AS ANNOUNCED IN 1997. SINCE THEN, SEVERAL OTHER MAMMALS HAVE ALSO BEEN SUCCESSFULLY CLONED.

Cloning a mammal leads to the question of whether or not humans will ever be cloned. As more and more different types of mammals are successfully cloned, it certainly seems possible. Cloning humans would give couples who have had trouble having a baby a new way to have a child. However, cloned embryos often die during the process, and if they do survive, the animals sometimes have health problems. For instance, Dolly died in 2003, living several years less than the average sheep. There are also concerns that a cloned human would not be treated as an individual. Several countries have gone so far as to ban human cloning.

Another possibility in the area of human cloning is reproducing certain organs. This can be done using special cells called stem cells. Scientists have already been able to grow new skin for burn victims. Some day they may be able to grow hearts, livers, or other body parts to help people who need new ones.

Learning more about genetics has opened up many possibilities, both exciting and frightening. In a few years, it is possible that all new parents will receive a copy of their baby's DNA. This will help doctors detect and cure inherited diseases or allergies. It could also help identify learning difficulties that are genetic. Doctors may some day be able to introduce into a body genes that produce enzymes which a person cannot produce because of a faulty inherited gene. Certain cancer drugs are available now that block the chemical signals that tell the cancer to grow. Some day these drugs may eliminate current cancer therapies like surgery and chemotherapy.

On the other hand, if a person's DNA indicates a greater risk for heart disease or cancer, that person may have trouble getting insurance. An inherited tendency toward mental illness or alcoholism might cause schools or employers to be prejudiced against a person. Would you want to know your DNA?

The strides made in genetics over the last century have been truly amazing. Sir Isaac Newton once said, "If I have done great things, it is only because I have stood on the shoulders of giants." In science, great discoveries are made by building on the successes of others. Watson, Crick, and Wilkins discovered the structure of DNA by studying what others before them had learned. They, in turn, made a discovery that allowed later scientists to unlock more of the secrets of life.

CHAPTER TWO

AN UNLIKELY TEAM

James Watson was born on April 6, 1928, in Chicago, Illinois. He was a small, unathletic child. From an early age, he developed the habit of always saying what he considered to be the truth, even if it hurt other people's feelings. This made him something of a loner. He was very bright and, as a child, once competed on the Quiz Kids radio program. He lasted through three sessions before missing a question on Shakespeare.[1]

In 1943, at the age of fifteen, James headed to the University of Chicago to study zoology. He was particularly interested in ornithology, the study of birds. Four years later, he graduated and went on to graduate school at the University of Indiana. At the beginning of his studies there he was still interested in birds, avoiding any kind of chemistry or physics courses. He planned to pursue a career as a naturalist.

In his senior year at the University of Chicago, Watson had become interested in genes. In graduate school he was greatly influenced by the book *What Is Life?* The author, Erwin Schrodinger, a physicist, tried to apply his findings in physics to molecular biology. Although Schrodinger believed that the gene was the most important part of the study of biology, no one was quite certain what a gene looked like or how it worked.

Watson decided that genetics, not ornithology, would be his field. He began to study with the microbiologist Salvador Luria, who had founded the Phage Group. The Phage Group was an organization whose members were interested in how viruses reproduced, or replicated themselves. Viruses are the simplest living things and thus provide the easiest way to study genes. The simplest kinds of viruses are called *bacteriophages*, or just *phages*. Watson saw Luria's work as a way to learn more about genetics. With Luria as his advisor, he began to work on a doctoral thesis that dealt with the study of phages.[2]

In 1950 Watson received a fellowship to study in Copenhagen, Denmark, with biochemist Herman Kalcker, who was interested in DNA. Watson hoped to pursue his own interests in genetics, but two factors interfered with his plan. First, Watson found he was still completely uninterested in the chemistry involved in the work Kalcker was doing. Second, he could not understand Kalcker's English.[3] Instead, he found himself working more frequently with another Danish scientist, Ole Maaloe, who was doing phage experiments similar to what Watson had been working on back in the United States.

Watson was more productive with Maaloe, collecting enough data on phages to publish an article about their work. However, he felt slightly guilty that he was not doing

JAMES WATSON AT AGE TEN.

the work he was supposed to be doing according to the terms of his fellowship.[4] He also was not learning any of the biochemistry he would need to pursue a career in genetics. But Watson was pleased when Kalcker proposed that he accompany him on a trip to Naples, Italy. Kalcker had decided to spend two months at the Zoological Station there. This trip eventually led Watson to his work at the Cavendish Laboratory with Francis Crick.

During a scientific meeting in Naples, Watson met Maurice Wilkins, a physicist who had become interested in biology. Wilkins was working at King's College in London, trying to figure out the structure of DNA. The method he was using was called X-ray diffraction photography. He gave a talk in which he showed a slide of one of the photographs he had taken of DNA. Watson was excited about this photograph. He had felt that most of the other scientists' work at this particular meeting lacked concrete facts. Wilkins' work stood out from the rest.[5]

When Watson learned that there was another X-ray diffraction unit at the Cavendish Laboratory, he immediately began looking for a way to work there. He wrote to his old adviser, Salvador Luria, to tell him about his new interest. A short time later, Luria attended a meeting in Ann Arbor, Michigan, where he met John Kendrew, who worked at the Cavendish. When Kendrew told Luria that the lab was understaffed, Luria told him about Watson.[6]

By this time, it was early August 1950, and Watson's fellowship was due to expire in a month. He applied to the Merck Foundation, which had given him the funding to go to Copenhagen, and asked to transfer to Cambridge.[7] Since he had had no trouble moving around before, Watson

JAMES WATSON AT ELEVEN YEARS OLD WITH HIS SISTER, ELIZABETH, AND THEIR FATHER, JAMES, SR.

assumed that the funding would come through. He went ahead and moved to Cambridge. A few weeks later he received a letter saying the foundation was not willing to support his new work. Fortunately, he had saved some money from his days in Copenhagen. John Kendrew offered him a room in his house, and Watson was able to begin work.

After his first day at the Cavendish, Watson knew he had found the right place. Although most of the scientists were working on the structures of proteins, he was delighted to meet Francis Crick, who was equally interested in solving the structure of DNA. They were both closely

AN EIGHTEEN-YEAR-OLD JAMES WATSON STANDS OUTSIDE HIS HOME IN CHICAGO, ILLINOIS, IN 1946.

following the work of Linus Pauling, who had recently published an article on the structure of proteins.

Although Crick was twelve years older than Watson, he had also recently changed career paths and was still working on his Ph.D. Known for his loud laugh and ready opinions and advice on the solution to any scientific problem, Crick had had an undistinguished career until that point. James Watson, the bird-watcher who disliked chemistry, and Francis Crick, the physicist-turned-biologist, seemed an unlikely team to work on such a complicated problem as solving the structure of DNA.

CHAPTER THREE

A MUTUAL GOAL

When Francis Crick was born in Northampton, England, in 1916, his mother told her sister to carry him to the attic of their house. She was somewhat superstitious and had heard that this would make her son "rise to the top."[1] Francis was the oldest of two sons born to Harry and Annie Crick.

Francis's mother obviously had great ambitions for him. As he was growing up, both of his parents tried to nurture his talents. Although they had limited money, they bought him a set of children's encyclopedias which Francis enjoyed reading. The books contained information on art, literature, and history, but Francis was particularly drawn to anything about science. Before long, Francis began trying many experiments at home, including blowing up bottles using electricity. Eventually, his parents ruled that Francis could only blow up his bottles in a bucket of water.[2]

Francis won a scholarship to Mill Hill School, a boarding school in North London, where he got a solid background in science, particularly physics. Then he went on to University College, London. When he graduated with a degree in physics, he applied to do research that would lead to a Ph.D. Because his professor did not think he was particularly capable, Crick was assigned the dullest task the professor could come up with: making a copper sphere to test water viscosity (how fluids behave). Crick, who was anxious to do something concrete in science after years of merely learning about it, actually enjoyed the problem.[3]

Crick was relieved of this task when World War II broke out. He was drafted into the British Admiralty, a government department that directs the Navy, and put to work designing explosives such as mines. In 1940, he married Ruth Dodd, and the couple had a son, Michael. After the war ended, he was uncertain about what career path to pursue. Although he had worked in science for several years, nothing had really sparked his interest. He decided he wanted to do research but did not know what subject to choose.

To help figure out what interested him most, Crick developed the "gossip test." While he was still working for the Admiralty, he found himself telling his coworkers about recent developments in antibiotics that he found exciting. He realized he did not really know much about the science; he was just gossiping about it the way that people gossip about what interests them. He started thinking about which science topics excited him enough to gossip about. He came up with two: the borderline between the living and the nonliving, and the workings of the brain. He found these two topics interesting because they both dealt with mysteries—the mystery of life and the mystery of consciousness.[4]

Two other events helped him in his career decision. First, he heard a lecture by Linus Pauling that got him thinking about doing chemical research. He also read Erwin Schrodinger's *What Is Life?*—the same book that influenced James Watson. Crick was interested in the way Schrodinger applied physics to the study of genetics. Like Watson, this book helped Crick decide to enter the field of genetics research.[5]

Unfortunately, like Watson, Crick knew very little about the biology, organic chemistry, and crystallography he would need to pursue genetics. He spent the next couple of years studying these subjects. In 1949 he went to Cambridge University, where he began working at Strangeways Research Laboratory. By this time, he was divorced, and in 1949 he married a Frenchwoman named Odile Speed.

Two years later, he moved to the Cavendish Laboratory. The Medical Research Council, which had been supporting his research, was opening a new unit headed by Max Perutz and Sir Lawrence Bragg. It was while working there that Crick became interested in the problem of DNA. It was also at Cavendish that Crick's path crossed with James Watson for the first time.

"I have never seen Francis Crick in a modest mood," Watson later reported. "From my first day in the lab I knew I would not leave Cambridge for a long time. Departing would be idiocy, for I had immediately discovered the fun of talking to Francis Crick."[6]

Watson and Crick hit it off almost immediately, although they tended to drive some of their other colleagues crazy. Both of them loved to talk and would spend

FRANCIS CRICK AND JAMES WATSON (LEFT TO RIGHT) WALK ALONG THE STREETS OF LONDON.

many hours thinking out loud about their ideas concerning DNA. They enjoyed going for long walks together and talking over lunch at their favorite pub, The Eagle. They talked so much at Cavendish that they were soon given their own office. Although they were officially working on different projects, it soon became evident that they were both passionate about solving the riddle of DNA's structure.

CHAPTER FOUR

PERSONALITY CLASH

Watson and Crick would eventually share the Nobel Prize with Maurice Wilkins, whom Watson met in Naples at a scientific conference shortly before moving to England to work at the Cavendish Laboratory.

Maurice Hugh Frederick Wilkins was born in Pongaroa, New Zealand, on December 15, 1916. His parents were both from Ireland, and his father, Edgar, was a doctor in the School Medical Service. Although Edgar was interested in research, he had very little chance to do any.

When Maurice was six, his family moved to England. He was sent to King Edward's School in Birmingham. From there he went to Cambridge University, where he studied physics and got his undergraduate degree in 1938. He went on to Birmingham University for graduate work, where he worked as a research assistant to John Randall on the development of radar and earned a Ph.D. two years later.

During World War II, Wilkins continued to work with

Randall on radar projects, then moved on to work with M.L.E. Oliphant. In 1943, Oliphant's group moved to Berkeley, California. There Wilkins became part of the Manhattan Project, working on the development of the atomic bomb. This experience led Wilkins to become a vocal opponent of nuclear weapons, which he continues to be to this day.[1]

After the war, in 1945, Wilkins returned to Great Britain, to Saint Andrews University in Scotland. During this time there was government support for physicists like Wilkins entering the field of biology. Physicists had had a large influence on the outcome of the war and there was a belief that they could use their talents to work on some of the biological problems that were at the heart of medical research.[2]

At Saint Andrews, Wilkins' old boss John Randall was working with X-ray crystallography, applying it to biology. The biophysics lab was moved to King's College in London in 1946, and Wilkins became a member of the staff there as part of the new Medical Research Council Biophysics Research Unit. After working on a variety of projects, he began trying to learn the structure of DNA using X-ray diffraction.[3]

It was during this time that Wilkins first met Francis Crick. While Crick was trying to decide which career path to follow, his wartime supervisor, H.S.W. Massey, suggested Crick get together with Wilkins. Massey, a physicist, had worked with Wilkins on the Manhattan Project. He felt that Crick might be interested in talking to another physicist who was entering the field of biology. Although Crick decided he was not interested in the work Wilkins was pursuing at that time, they did become friends. They were both about the same age, interested in similar areas of science, and even looked alike. Since Crick's mother's maiden name was Wilkins, he even wondered at one time if they might be distantly related![4]

In 1950, Wilkins and his colleague Raymond Gosling produced the first images of DNA. Gosling's work was continued the following year by a new member of the lab, Rosalind Franklin. Born in 1920, Franklin was the daughter of Ellis Franklin and Muriel Waley Franklin, members of two prominent British Jewish families. When Rosalind was fifteen, she decided she wanted to pursue a career in science. This was so difficult for a woman that even her father, who was very supportive of Rosalind, doubted that it was a worthwhile pursuit.[5] However, Rosalind persisted, and in 1938, she entered Cambridge University, where she earned her undergraduate degree in chemistry, and then went on to graduate work.

After a year of research at Cambridge, Franklin left for a position at the British Coal Utilization Research Association (CURA). She remained there for five years and did important work on the structure of coal. This involved working on a scale so small that some of her measurements were done using a helium molecule as a unit of measure.[6] She was very successful at CURA, publishing several papers on her work.

After the war, Franklin was restless and looking for a new direction.[7] She decided to take a position at the Laboratoire Central des Services Chimiques de l'Etat in Paris. She spent three happy years there. France was much more open to women in the sciences than was England.

ROSALIND FRANKLIN WAS ONE OF THE KEY CONTRIBUTORS TO THE DEVELOPMENT OF AN ACCURATE MODEL OF DNA.

Franklin made many friends and was able to pursue interesting work, including learning X-ray diffraction techniques.

Although she enjoyed her time in Paris very much, Franklin decided to move back to England to King's College in London to apply her expertise in X-ray diffraction to the field of biology. In 1951, she was given a Turner-Newall Research Fellowship to come to King's to set up an X-ray diffraction unit in the laboratory. Although she was not hired specifically to study DNA, that was the problem that most interested her.[8]

From the very beginning of her time at King's, there was friction between Rosalind Franklin and Maurice Wilkins. The cause of this is unclear. King's at that time was inhospitable to women. For instance, all the men on the faculty ate together, while the women ate with the students. This may have caused Franklin to feel like an outsider. However, since she got along with other colleagues, there seems to have been a more specific personality clash between her and Wilkins.

Franklin was very passionate about science and enjoyed debating, while Wilkins was quieter and more likely to walk away from an argument. When she was first hired, there were two incidents that may have contributed to their conflict. Wilkins was away when a meeting was held to discuss Franklin's role in the DNA work, so he did not get to add his input. He may have felt slighted because of this. Also, Franklin solved a fairly simple problem within her first few weeks at the lab, and afterward Wilkins felt she began to act very superior about it.[9]

The exact cause of the differences will probably never be

known. Most likely, Wilkins and Franklin simply had personalities that clashed. Whatever the reason, they did their best to avoid working with one another. In the world of science, where collaboration is important, this did not help their cause of finding the structure of DNA.

CHAPTER FIVE

WHAT IS DNA?

Francis Crick, James Watson, Maurice Wilkins, and Rosalind Franklin were all working to find the structure of deoxyribonucleic acid, or DNA. Why was this important? To learn the answer, it is necessary to look at the history of genetics—the science of how certain traits are passed from parents to their offspring. From ancient times, people have observed that parents and their children look similar, whether they are humans, animals, or plants. The reason for this, however, remained a mystery until the beginning of the twentieth century. It was then that the work of an unlikely scientist was made public.

Gregor Mendel was born in 1822 in what was then called the Austro-Hungarian Empire. His parents were peasants and, although Mendel had a great thirst for learning, his family could not afford much of an education for him. Entering the priesthood was the only way he could continue his education. He became a priest and entered a monastery in Brünn, now part of the Czech Republic.

He worked in the garden there and began painstaking observations of its edible pea plants. He observed seven characteristics in the plants, such as height, flower color, and the shape of their seeds. By crossbreeding plants with different traits, he was able to make observations about the results.

For instance, in one of his experiments he fertilized short plants with pollen from tall plants. Then he planted the seeds that formed. Even though the plants from these seeds had one tall parent and one short parent, the seeds produced all tall plants. When he crossbred two of these tall plants, he found that only three-quarters of the offspring were tall and the rest were short. Mendel believed that each trait he was studying was caused by two factors, one contributed by each parent. Today we call these factors genes.

When the tall and short plants were bred together, the offspring contained both a tall factor and a short factor. Mendel's conclusion was that the tall factor was dominant. When the two offspring were combined, sometimes the non-dominant, or recessive, factors from two plants would combine. There were four possible combinations of factors: two tall, a short and a tall, a tall and a short, and two short. Since the tallness factor was dominant, three-fourths of the plants, or those that contained at least one tallness factor, would be tall. In one-quarter of the plants, the shortness factors would be present from both parent plants, producing a short plant.

Mendel conducted more than 20,000 experiments. He was able to show why traits sometimes skip generations (because they are recessive traits, and both parents must contribute the recessive trait to have it show up in the offspring), and why different children of the same parents have different traits (each one has a unique combination of the parents' traits). In 1866 he published his findings in the magazine of the Natural Science Society at Brünn. Since this was not a well-known publication, few scientists read his article.

In addition, Mendel shared his work with Karl von Naegeli, a leading German botanist who did not agree with his conclusions. Although Mendel had done exhaustive experiments with his pea plants, von Naegeli suggested he do more with another plant called hawkweed. Unfortunately, the hawkweed studies did not match the pea pod studies, and Mendel became discouraged and gave up on this work. When he died in 1884, his work was unknown. It was not until around 1900, when the field of genetics became established, that his findings became more widely known and accepted.

Other scientists working at the end of the nineteenth century also made discoveries and observations that would be relevant to James Watson's work. In 1869, Friedrich Miescher, a Swiss biochemist, observed what he called "nuclein" in his work with blood cells. This was what we now call DNA. Ten years later, Walther Flemming, a German scientist, discovered "chromatin," a part of the nuclei of cells that we now know as chromosomes.

There were a number of new discoveries about genetics in the first half of the twentieth century. During the early 1900s, the American scientist Thomas Hunt Morgan did a series of experiments with fruit flies. Since these flies reproduce every fourteen days, it is easy to observe characteristics of several generations over a short period of time.

GREGOR MENDEL IS WIDELY CONSIDERED TO BE THE FATHER OF THE
SCIENTIFIC FIELD OF GENETICS.

Through his experiments, Morgan showed that fruit flies have four groups of linked genes. This means that he was able to group the flies' characteristics to see that there were four groups that often occurred together from one generation to the next. He concluded that this meant that fruit fly cells contain four chromosomes. (By comparison, human cells have forty-six chromosomes).

Morgan knew from previous work done by Walther Flemming that chromosome groups can be split into identical halves. These groups scatter through the cell and then recombine. By observing the traits of generations of fruit flies, Morgan concluded that some genes on the same chromosome re-assort, or become redistributed, while others remain linked. He also deduced that the genes that were farthest from each other were most likely to re-assort. From this, he was able to begin to work on a gene map of one of the fruit fly's chromosomes. He and his colleagues mapped more than 200 genes on the fruit fly chromosome.

During the 1920s, a scientist named Fred Griffiths, working in London, carried out some experiments with mice to learn about pneumcoocci, the bacteria that causes pneumonia. By studying pneumococci cells under the microscope, he learned that they were smooth and shiny when they were infectious (able to cause the disease), and dull and rough when they were noninfectious. When the smooth cells were heated, they were killed and became rough.

Griffiths found that if he injected mice with rough cells or heat-killed smooth cells, the mice did not become infected with pneumonia. However, if he injected both types of cells, they did become infected. When he examined

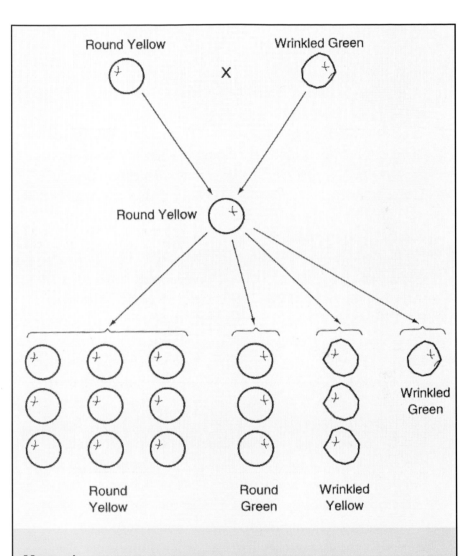

Round Yellow   X   Wrinkled Green

Round Yellow

Round
Yellow

Round
Green

Wrinkled
Yellow

Wrinkled
Green

the mice, he found that the two types of cells had somehow formed smooth cells. This change would be passed down to the next generation of cells. A chemical transformation had occurred.

In 1944, Oswald Avery, an American scientist working at the Rockefeller Institute in New York, set out to determine the "transforming principle" that had caused the changes Griffiths found. By doing a chemical analysis of pneumococci samples, he discovered there were no proteins in the transforming material. He found that the material was high in nucleic acids, and eventually concluded that it was DNA that caused the transformation.

By the 1940s more had been discovered about the mysterious substance DNA. While chromosomes could be seen with microscopes, DNA remained invisible. However, P.A.T. Levene, another scientist at the Rockefeller Institute, discovered that DNA was made up of four chemical bases: adenine, guanine, cytosine, and thymine (usually simply referred to as A, G, C, and T). At first, he thought that the amounts of each base varied and that these bases would carry genetic information. Eventually, though, he found that DNA contained what appeared to be equal amounts of the four bases. He concluded that DNA most likely did not carry genetic information. Many scientists believed that this information was carried by protein in the chromosome.[1]

Unfortunately, although Levene and Avery were colleagues at the Rockefeller Institute, they did not get along very well. Levene dismissed Avery's research, concluding that DNA was not an important factor in transmitting genetic information. Eventually, however, further investigation into the DNA molecule showed that it was made up of

FRED GRIFFITHS' EXPERIMENTS WITH MICE IN THE 1920S LED TO A BETTER UNDERSTANDING OF THE BACTERIA THAT CAUSES INFECTIOUS DISEASES. LABORATORY MICE HAVE BEEN VERY IMPORTANT IN THE DEVELOPMENT OF MODERN BIOLOGICAL SCIENCE.

a backbone made of sugar molecules connected together. One of the four bases, A, G, C, or T, was attached to each sugar molecule. This meant that DNA was a large molecule, capable of carrying genetic information. Levene was forced to reluctantly recognize the importance of DNA.[2]

Erwin Chargaff, a chemist working at Columbia University, made two more important discoveries about DNA. He found that, contrary to Levene's research, there were not equal amounts of the four bases in the DNA molecule. Instead he found that:

A+G = C+T

A=T

G=C

These became known as Chargaff's rules and would later prove important in Watson and Crick's research.

This was all that was known about DNA when Watson and Crick began their work. The two big questions about DNA were: how did it carry genetic information and how did it pass along that information when cells divided? The key to those questions seemed to lie in figuring out the structure of DNA.

CHAPTER SIX

EARLY
SETBACKS

Although the chemist Linus Pauling worked thousands of miles away from the Cavendish Laboratory, his influence was strongly felt by the scientists working there. Pauling was a chemist who had received his Ph.D. from the California Institute of Technology (Cal Tech) in Pasadena, California. He had remained at Cal Tech, and would eventually go on to win the 1954 Nobel Prize in chemistry. His work involved the links between atoms in complex molecules, called chemical bonds. Shortly before James Watson joined Cavendish, Pauling had dramatically unveiled his idea for the structure of proteins. Pauling believed that the protein structure, and probably many other biological structures like DNA, was a spiral shape called a helix.

The laboratory technique that both Pauling and Rosalind Franklin used—and that Watson hoped to learn how to use was called X ray crystallography. Two pioneers in crystallography were Sir William Bragg and his son, Sir Lawrence Bragg, who was head of the Cavendish

Laboratory. Crystallography is used to look at objects that are smaller than the wavelength of light. X-rays have a wavelength 5,000 to 10,000 times shorter than light, which makes their wavelength about the same as the distance between atoms in crystals.

When a beam of X-rays is passed through a crystal, the X-rays are diffracted (or spread out) by the crystal's atoms into a pattern which can then be photographed. By studying the pattern in the photograph, it is possible to figure out the structure of the crystal.[1] Although the photographs do not look like much to the untrained observer, a trained scientist can use mathematical analysis to create a three-dimensional model from them. These techniques were used at first to study metals and minerals. They were later expanded to include biological substances that form crystals. Because most molecules that interest biologists are very large, using X-ray diffraction to study them was particularly difficult.[2]

Although scientists at Cavendish were not officially investigating the structure of DNA, James Watson was hoping to learn more about X-ray diffraction techniques to study it. When he arrived at Cavendish, he was delighted to learn that Francis Crick was also interested in the structure of DNA.[3] Soon Crick and Watson were having lengthy discussions about it. They began by studying Linus Pauling's work on the a-helix, the structure for protein that he had proposed. Watson soon got some ideas about their own work.

> I soon was taught that Pauling's accomplishment was a product of common sense, not the result of complicated mathematical reasoning. Equations occasionally crept

LIKE WATSON, NOBEL PRIZE-WINNING SCIENTIST LINUS PAULING WAS INTERESTED IN DISCOVERING THE TRUE STRUCTURE OF DNA.

into his argument, but in most cases words would have sufficed. The key to Linus's success was his reliance on the simple laws of structural chemistry. The a-helix had not been found by only staring at X-ray pictures; the essential trick, instead, was to ask which atoms like to sit next to each other. In place of pencil and paper, the main working tools were a set of molecular models superficially resembling the toys of preschool children. We could thus see no reason why we should not solve DNA in the same way.[4]

DNA seemed to be a more complex structure than the a-helix. In the a-helix, the helix is made up of a single chain of amino acids held together by hydrogen bonds between groups on the same chain. The DNA molecule appeared to be thicker, which meant it probably had more than one chain.

It was a little awkward for Watson and Crick to show much interest in the DNA problem. The British scientific community was fairly small, and most scientists knew what others in their fields were working on. It was common knowledge that the Cavendish lab was working on protein structures while scientists at King's College were focusing on DNA. This was not an official assignment but more of a "gentlemen's agreement."[5] Watson and Crick were far too interested in DNA to abandon it, but the situation made it difficult to collaborate with Maurice Wilkins and Rosalind Franklin.

Before long, Francis Crick had some success in the DNA work. He read an article in which a scientist named V. Vand described a general theory for testing models that contained helices. He immediately saw errors in this theory and decided to see if he could come up with the correct theory. One of his colleagues at Cavendish, Bill Cochran, began to work on it as well. Although Cochran did not usually work on the large biological molecules, he was considered the best crystallographer in the lab.

Crick spent one morning working on the problem, so absorbed in mathematical equations that he was uncharacteristically quiet. That afternoon he went home with a headache, but could not stop working on the equations. Finally, he believed he had found the solution. The next morning, he arrived excitedly at Cavendish, where Bill Cochran informed him that he had found a solution, too. They compared their work and found that, although they had used different mathematical work, they had arrived at the same solution. Soon they had an article published with this work in the scientific journal *Nature*.[6]

The next milestone in the search for the DNA model was a seminar held by Rosalind Franklin in which she summarized the work she had done. Of the Cavendish colleagues, only Watson attended. This turned out to be unfortunate, since he never took notes at lectures. When he reported back to Crick, he discovered that he was unsure of the water content of the DNA samples that Franklin had measured. This proved to be a crucial mistake.

Crick used the information Watson gave him and combined it with the theory he had recently published with Bill Cochran. He believed that based on his information and research there could only be a few solutions to the DNA problem.[7] Immediately, Watson and Crick began building models to see if they could figure out the structure.

While the work at King's College was mostly based on X-ray diffraction photographs, Crick and Watson were partial to model making. In model making, a structure is put together and then rearranged until all information, from X-ray diffraction photos and other sources, has been taken into account. Both methods had been used to understand the structures of various substances. The earliest X-ray diffraction work had been done with very simple structures like that of sodium chloride. Many times these structures could be created by simply studying the X-ray diffraction photographs. In more complicated structures, like DNA, both methods were used to come up with a solution.[8] Some scientists, such as Linus Pauling, preferred model making, while others, like Rosalind Franklin, believed that X-ray diffraction was a better way to solve problems.

Within a few days, Crick and Watson had put together a model. From what Rosalind Franklin had said at her seminar, they believed that the DNA model was a helix with between two and four chains. Their model had three chains with the bases (A, C, T, and G) on the outside of the helices. Crick called Maurice Wilkins to see if he would be interested in coming to Cambridge to take a look at their model. Wilkins said he would be down the next day with several colleagues, including Rosalind Franklin.

Crick was prepared for an exciting meeting at which he would first explain the importance of his helix theory and then show the model he and Watson had created. Unfortunately, things did not go as planned. When the model was displayed, Rosalind Franklin raised several objections. Watson later reported on the meeting:

> Most annoyingly, her objections were not mere perversity; at this stage the embarrassing fact came out that my recollection of the water content of [Franklin's] DNA

JAMES WATSON IN PARIS SOME TIME IN THE 1950s.

samples could not be right. The awkward truth became apparent that the correct DNA model must contain at least ten times more water than was found in our model.... [T]here was no escaping the conclusion that our argument was soft. As soon as the possibility arose that much more water was involved, the number of potential DNA models alarmingly increased.[9]

The meeting ended uncomfortably. With the model not only so obviously wrong, but also based on clearly incorrect information, it had been a waste of time for Franklin and Wilkins to come to Cambridge from London.

The whole incident almost ended Crick's involvement with DNA. Sir Lawrence Bragg had had trouble with Crick before. When he heard about the meeting with the scientists from King's College, he called Crick into his office, where he reprimanded him for working on a project that supposedly belonged to King's. The Medical Research Council was funding both the protein work at Cavendish and the DNA research at King's. Bragg believed that if the Council found out that there was duplicate work going on at both labs, they would stop funding any work at Cavendish. There were many British people who felt the whole Medical Research Council was a waste of money. In the difficult years after World War II, they felt the government should be funding more practical projects.[10] Bragg's final words to Crick were to forbid him from doing any more work on DNA.

CHAPTER SEVEN

A KEY INSIGHT

The outlook for the discovery of DNA's structure in England looked gloomy as 1951 drew to a close. The Cambridge meeting with the group from King's College had resulted in cooler relations between the two labs. Francis Crick was back at work on his thesis, while James Watson had decided to work on research on the tobacco mosaic virus (TMV). However, since an important part of TMV was nucleic acid, Watson used this work to continue pursuing his interest in DNA. Also, Sir Lawrence Bragg's order to discontinue work on DNA did not extend to lunches. Often, DNA was the topic of conversation when Crick and Watson met for lunch at their favorite pub, the Eagle.

TMV is made up of a form of nucleic acid called *ribonucleic acid*, or *RNA*. The focus of Watson's research was on whether the virus had a helical structure. Based on work that was done in the 1930s, he believed that the virus was made up of a central RNA core surrounded by small identical units of protein.[1] Watson wanted to learn if the units of protein were arranged in a helix around the RNA center.

To do this, he needed to see some X-ray pictures. Hugh Huxley, a colleague at the Cavendish, offered to teach him how to take the pictures he needed. By tilting the virus at an angle to the X-ray beam, it was easier to see the helix—if there was one.[2] A new machine using a rotating anode X-ray tube had just been installed at the lab, which allowed Watson to take twenty times as many pictures as he could have done before. He worked late into the night for months trying to get the pictures he needed. They eventually revealed that the structure of the virus was indeed a helix.

When Watson showed the photographs to Crick, they re-ignited Crick's determination to work on DNA. He began having more conversations with his coworkers on the subject. One evening, he was talking with a chemist named John Griffiths. The two had just attended a talk by an astronomer on "The Perfect Cosmological Principle." Crick began wondering aloud about "The Perfect Biological Principle." His idea was that this principle would be the ability of a gene to be copied during cell division. Griffiths had a different idea about how the gene would be duplicated. His idea was that to reproduce itself, the gene must form a complementary image that would fit with the original like a key fits a lock.

Although Griffiths and Crick disagreed on the hypothesis of how this would be done, they both believed that the key to it would be to measure the attractive forces between the bases (A, C, G, and T) in the molecule. Griffiths believed he could measure these forces. He and Crick

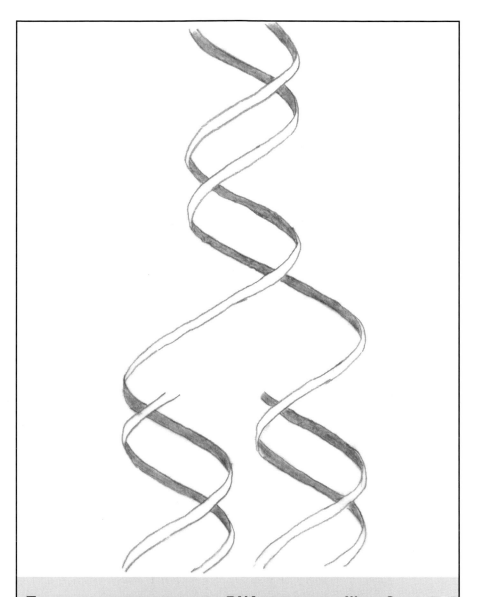

THE ABOVE DIAGRAM SHOWS HOW DNA REPRODUCES. WHEN CRICK HAD FIRST CORRECTLY DEDUCED HOW DNA REPRODUCES, IT WAS A KEY BREAKTHROUGH.

believed that if Griffiths's theory of complementary bases were right, he would find attractive forces between different bases. If Crick were right, he would find the attractive forces between identical bases.[3]

A few days later, Crick met up with Griffiths again. Griffiths said that his studies suggested that the bases adenine and thymine should stick together in the molecule, as should guanine and cytosine. Crick saw this information as the key to DNA's replication. He pictured a model of DNA in which the helical strand would split in two, creating two strands identical to the one from which they had parted.[4] In a brilliant flash of insight, Crick had come up with the correct method of DNA reproduction.

CHAPTER EIGHT

THE RACE FOR DNA

During the next several months, little progress was made on understanding the DNA molecule. Both Watson and Crick were working on other projects. After learning a little more about the molecule's four bases, there was no other new information to inspire them to start building new models. Then something happened that motivated them to redouble their efforts.

A new scientist had started working at Cavendish. His name was Peter Pauling, and he was none other than the son of the famous Linus Pauling. One day, Peter Pauling shared a letter from his father with Watson and Crick. Watson remembered:

> In addition to routine family gossip was the long-feared news that Linus now had a structure for DNA. No details were given of what he was up to, and so each time the letter passed between Francis and me the greater was our frustration. Francis then began pacing up and down the room thinking aloud. . . . As long as Linus had not

---

told us the answer, we should get equal credit if we announced at the same time.[1]

Unfortunately, Watson and Crick were short on any new information to work with to make their own progress.

A couple months went by with no more word from Linus Pauling on DNA. Then a letter arrived saying Pauling had a manuscript on DNA he would be sending shortly. Sure enough, two copies arrived at Cavendish, one sent to Sir Lawrence Bragg and one to Peter Pauling. In the manuscript, Linus Pauling described a model with a sugar-phosphate backbone surrounded by three helices. It was, in fact, quite similar to the incorrect model Watson and Crick had put together the previous year.

At first Watson was bitterly disappointed, thinking that if he and Crick had pursued their original model, they might have come up with the correct DNA structure.[2] But as he looked at the manuscript more closely, he realized that Pauling had made a couple of basic chemistry errors that made it impossible for his model to be correct. He had

PETER PAULING (LEFT) AND JAMES WATSON IN WATSON'S HARVARD OFFICE.

forgotten to give the phosphate groups in his chain any ionization, which meant they would not have an electrical charge to hold them together. Without the ionization, his model was not even an acid. Watson showed it to Crick who agreed that it could not be right. The two of them felt they still had a chance, but there was not much time. In about six weeks, Pauling's paper would be published and the error brought to his attention.

At that point, the Cavendish team got a break. Watson had visited London several days after reading Linus Pauling's work. While there, he stopped in to see Maurice Wilkins and told him about Pauling's error. As he often did, Wilkins then talked to Watson about his ongoing difficulties in working with Rosalind Franklin.

Franklin and her assistant, Raymond Gosling, had come up with a new way to photograph DNA. By increasing the humidity in the lab, they were able to create a form of DNA with a higher water content. They called this the B form. It resulted in the clearest pictures of DNA that had yet been taken. When Wilkins saw these photographs, he expressed interest in working with Franklin on her investigation.

Franklin had exploded at this idea, feeling that Wilkins was trying to elbow his way into work that she had had to do by herself.[3] They ended up having a fairly public argument, resulting in the director of their laboratory assigning the B form to Wilkins and the A form to Franklin.

During his meeting with Watson, Wilkins told him about the photographs of the B form that Franklin had taken. When Watson asked what these photos looked like, Wilkins went into the adjoining room and brought a copy

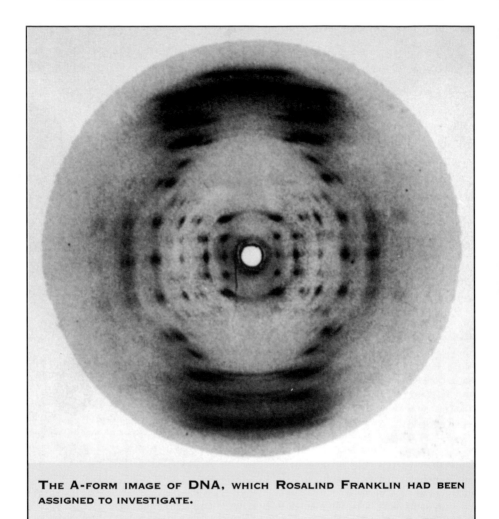

THE A-FORM IMAGE OF DNA, WHICH ROSALIND FRANKLIN HAD BEEN ASSIGNED TO INVESTIGATE.

to show him. "The instant I saw the picture my mouth fell open and my pulse began to race," reported Watson.

The pattern was unbelievably simpler than those obtained previously (A form). Moreover, the black cross of reflections which dominated the picture could arise only from a helical structure. With the A form, the argument for a helix was never straightforward, and considerable ambiguity existed as to exactly which type of helical structure was present. With the B form, however, mere inspection of its X-ray picture gave several of the vital helical parameters. Conceivably, after only a few minutes' calculations, the number of chains in the molecule could be fixed.[4]

Thus, not only did the photo clearly show a helical structure, but Watson believed he could figure out the number of chains that were in the helix.

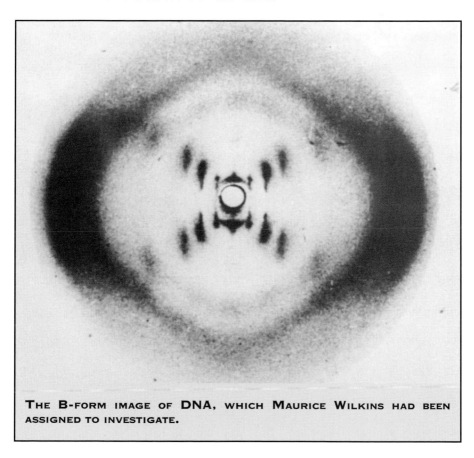

THE B-FORM IMAGE OF DNA, WHICH MAURICE WILKINS HAD BEEN ASSIGNED TO INVESTIGATE.

Watson asked Wilkins what the people at King's had done with the new data. Wilkins said one of his colleagues had been working on models that had three chains in the helix, but he had not had much success. Most of the scientists working at his lab believed the model had the bases at the center with the strands of the helix on the outside.

On the train back to Cambridge that night, Watson thought about the photograph he had seen. Although the King's scientists believed the model had three strands in the helix, their theory was based on the water content of DNA, which they admitted might be in great error. Watson decided he was going to build a model using a helix with two strands.[5] He decided that "Francis would have to agree. Even though he was a physicist, he knew that important biological objects come in pairs."[6]

CHAPTER NINE

THE
STRUCTURE
OF DNA

The next morning, Watson rushed to Max Perutz's office at Cavendish. It was Saturday, and Crick was still at home. Sir Lawrence Bragg was in Perutz's office when Watson told them about the news from King's College. He drew a sketch of his idea for a model, then mentioned that he was going to have a machinist start working with him on building it. When Bragg raised no objections, Watson knew he was in the clear to begin working.[1]

Building a model of DNA was no simple task. Imagine two combs, each about six feet long, that have to be twisted in a corkscrew and then lined up so that each tooth on one comb meets up with a tooth on the other comb. The exact length, position, and angle of each tooth must be calculated before starting. The width of these two combs together is less than two nanometers. (A nanometer is one-billionth part of a meter.) Furthermore, building the model involved deciding the angle between the spirals of the helix, whether it would be tightly coiled like a spring or more stretched out.[2]

Crick was enthusiastic about getting back to model building when he arrived later that day, even though he still was not convinced that any conclusive evidence existed to make a two-strand model instead of a three-strand one. A few days later, when the pieces had been built by the Cavendish machinist, Crick and Watson were ready to begin. After several days of futile attempts, Watson began to wonder if they had the wrong idea in putting the backbone made up of the bases on the inside of the model. He decided to experiment with models in which the backbone was on the outside.[3]

At this point, Watson and Crick got further evidence that they were on the right track. They had gotten a hold of Rosalind Franklin's measurements and their work checked out with hers. Franklin was unaware, however, that they had a copy of her work. They had gotten it from Max Perutz, who was a member of a committee set up by the Medical Research Council to coordinate biophysics research going on at the different labs it supported. The scientists working at the lab at King's College had each put together a detailed report of their accomplishments. Perutz gave his copy of Franklin's report to Watson and Crick, and Watson was relieved to see that he had correctly reported the data on the B form of DNA that Maurice Wilkins had shown him.[4]

The main problem then was figuring out how the bases fit together along the helices. Since the bases were of

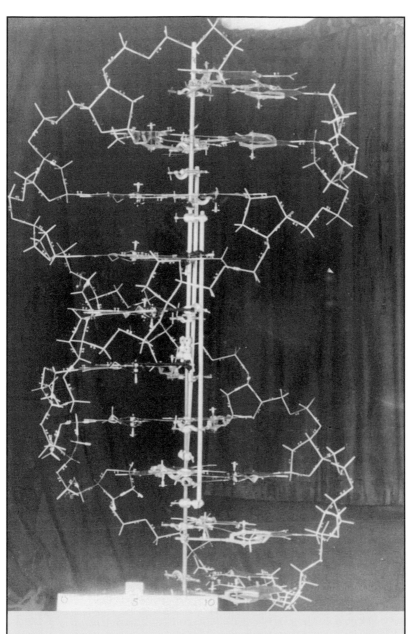

WATSON AND CRICK'S ORIGINAL DEMONSTRATION MODEL OF DNA.

different sizes, it seemed as though there was no way to get them to go together. If the bigger bases were touching, there would be a gap where the smaller bases lay next to each other. Another problem was the hydrogen bonds that would hold the bases together. If one or more hydrogen atoms on each base moved from one location to another, they would form hydrogen bonds between the bases. Until then, Crick and Watson had not thought the bases were held together with hydrogen bonds. As they studied the problem further and examined the X-ray photos, it became evident that hydrogen bonds probably did exist between the bases. Another way of solving the problem might be to figure out the rules about the behavior of these bonds.[5]

Watson's first idea about this was that the bases paired together, adenine with adenine, guanine with guanine, and so forth. Each pair would be held together by two hydrogen bonds. The pairs would come apart, with the whole structure splitting in two to reproduce itself. The only problem with this model was that adenine and guanine had different shapes from thymine and cytosine, which would make for a backbone that would go in and out. Despite this, Watson was excited about his new idea.[6]

Unfortunately, when he presented this idea at Cavendish the next day, he discovered it did not hold up. An organic chemist at the lab, Jerry Donohue, told Watson that the book he had been using to get the correct structures of the four bases was wrong. It would be almost impossible for a backbone to accommodate the new forms of these structures. Crick added that he did not like the model since it ignored Chargaff's rules about the bases that A=T and C=G. Watson went back to model making, cutting out

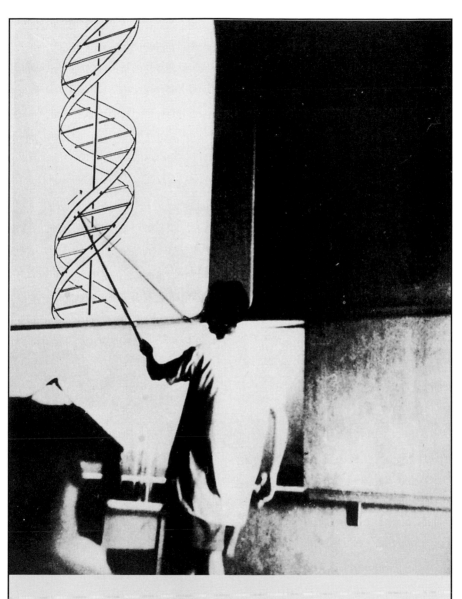

JAMES WATSON USES AN OVERHEAD PROJECTOR TO HELP EXPLAIN DNA'S DOUBLE-HELIX STRUCTURE DURING A LECTURE.

cardboard models of the bases since the ones he had ordered from the lab's shop were not ready yet.

The next day Watson arrived at the lab early in the morning and began working with the cardboard models. At first he went back to the like-with-like pairings, but then began trying other configurations. Suddenly he realized that the adenine-thymine pair was the same exact shape as the guanine-cystonine pair. They could both be held together by two hydrogen bonds. Jerry Donohue had arrived in the meantime, so Watson asked him to check his work. When Donohue said the pairings looked correct, Watson believed he had found the way the bases were arranged on the two helices. These pairings would make sense given Chargaff's rules and the identical sizes would make for an even backbone for the molecule.[7]

When Crick arrived, he was excited about Watson's cardboard models. At lunch in their favorite pub that day, to Watson's embarrassment, Crick told everyone within earshot that they had solved the secret of life.[8] Two days later the model parts were finished in the shop, and Watson and Crick could begin work on a three-dimensional model. Needless to say, Crick had given up any pretense of working on his thesis and was now working full-time on DNA. After all the work they had done with the cardboard models, it did not take long for them to complete a 3-D model. On March 7, 1953, after just five weeks of work, they were able to unveil their model to their colleagues at Cavendish.

Just as the model was being completed, a letter arrived from Maurice Wilkins saying he was about to start a serious attempt at model building. This made Watson and Crick

Watson and **Crick** stand before their original demonstration model of **DNA** shortly after the publication of their 1953 article in *Nature* which correctly detailed **DNA** structure.

uncomfortable about inviting him to look at their model, so their colleague John Kendrew called Wilkins and told him about the model.

Fortunately, when Wilkins came down to look, he immediately agreed that the model was correct, and showed no trace of bitterness that Watson and Crick had beaten him to a solution.[9] He offered to go back to King's College and compare their model to measurements using the X-ray diffraction photographs that he and Rosalind Franklin had taken.

Two days later, Wilkins called to say that their evidence strongly supported the model. Both he and Franklin wanted to write articles to go with the one Crick and Watson would publish to announce their discovery. Another scientist who was excited about their findings was Linus Pauling. When he heard of the model, he had no argument with it, and immediately expressed a wish to come see the model as soon as he could get to England.[10] A few weeks later he was able to visit, and gave his opinion again that the model was correct.

By that time, Watson and Crick had written an article for *Nature*, the British scientific journal, that began "We wish to suggest a structure for the salt of deoxyribose nucleic acid (DNA). This structure has novel features which are of considerable biological interest." To satisfy Crick, who wanted to write more about the biological importance of their discovery, the article included the sentence, "It has not escaped our notice that the specific pairing we have postulated immediately suggests a possible copying mechanism for genetic material."[11]

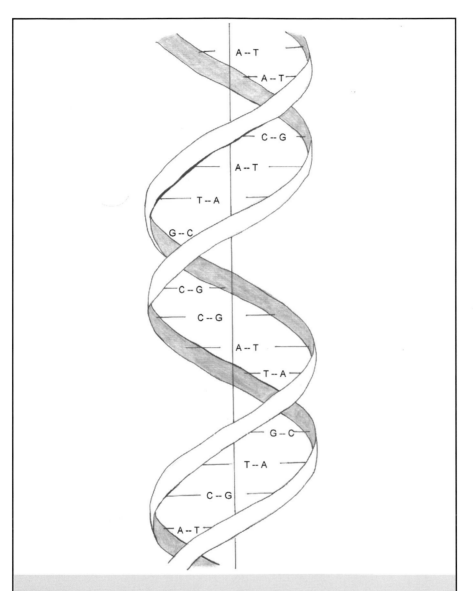

WATSON AND CRICK DESCRIBED THEIR DOUBLE-HELIX MODEL OF DNA AS RESEMBLING A "SPIRAL STAIRCASE," WITH THE BASE PAIRS THAT LINKED THE TWO HELICAL CHAINS AS THE "STEPS."

The nine-hundred-word article was sent in on April 2, 1953, with a strong cover letter from Sir Lawrence Bragg. It was published a few weeks later in the April 25 issue.

Although the secret of the structure of DNA had been discovered, it took scientists several years to understand its importance. Biophysics professor Alex Rich, who had been a student at the California Institute of Technology when the *Nature* article appeared, recalled that, "It was like a tree falling in the middle of the forest. It had no impact. Most places just ignored it."[12]

CHAPTER TEN

MOVING ON

Until the 1960s, there were almost no scientific papers written that referred to the original work published by Watson, Crick, Wilkins, and Franklin. It was not until scientists discovered how DNA duplicated itself and how its code was turned into proteins that the work became more accepted in the scientific community.[1] Watson, Crick, and Wilkins had to wait nine years to receive their Nobel Prize. Sadly, Rosalind Franklin did not survive to see her work recognized.

After their momentous discovery, Watson and Crick did not work together much longer. James Watson returned to the United States, working first at Cal Tech in Pasadena, California (Linus Pauling's home base), then moving on to Harvard University in 1955. He continued to do DNA research there. In 1965, he published the book *Molecular Biology of the Gene*, which is still considered one of the best textbooks on the topic. In 1968, he became director of the Cold Spring Harbor Laboratory in Long Island, New York. He continued to commute between Harvard and Cold Spring Harbor until 1976, when he became full-time director at Cold Spring Harbor.

Although Watson could give the impression of being absent-minded, he proved an effective fund-raiser and leader of this lab, which became one of the world's most important research institutions for molecular biology. Scientists working for Watson at Cold Spring Harbor became the first to identify cancer genes.[2] The laboratory also has a large educational component. Scientists come from all over the world to attend meetings, conferences, and courses on DNA and genetics.

In 1968, the same year Watson became director at Cold Spring Harbor, he published the book *The Double Helix*, the story of his and Crick's discovery of DNA. It became a best

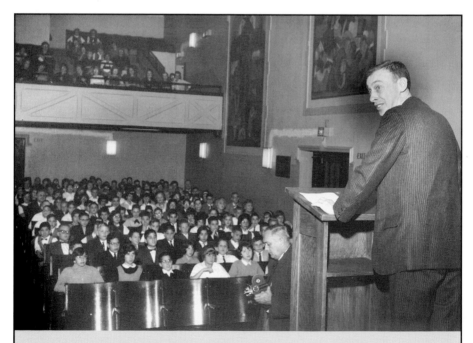

JAMES WATSON SPEAKS BEFORE AN ASSEMBLY OF HIGH SCHOOL STUDENTS IN CHICAGO.

seller and was hailed as one of the best accounts of scientific discovery written for non-scientists.

On March 28, 1968, James Watson married Elizabeth Lewis, his secretary at Cold Spring Harbor Lab. The couple would later have two sons, Rufus and Duncan.

In 1988, Watson took on an additional position as director of the National Center for Human Genome Research, part of the National Institutes for Health (NIH). His work there concerned the beginning of the human genome project. He resigned from the center in 1992. In 1994, Watson was named President of the Cold Spring Harbor Laboratory, a position he continues to hold to this day.

Francis Crick stayed at the Cavendish Laboratory for twenty more years. He and his wife Odile had two daughters, Gabrielle and Jacqueline, living in a house they named appropriately The Golden Helix. Eventually, he moved to the United States, going to the Salk Institute in San Diego, California, in 1977, at the age of sixty-one. He has continued to work with unusual and thought-provoking ideas. In 1981, he published a book, *Life Itself*, in which he argued that life on Earth originated in outer space. He also has investigated consciousness in humans and animals.[3]

Maurice Wilkins became Assistant Director of the Medical Research Council Unit at King's College in 1950 and Deputy Director in 1955. He was made Honorary Lecturer when a subdepartment of biophysics was formed at King's. This became a full Department of Biophysics in 1961. In 1959, Wilkins married Patricia Ann Chidgey. They have a daughter, Sarah, and a son, George.

Shortly after the discovery of DNA, Rosalind Franklin

LIZ AND JAMES WATSON ON THEIR WEDDING DAY.

left to work at a lab at Birkbeck College. Her supervisors at King's College did not allow her to continue working on DNA once she had left the lab there. Her work at Birkbeck focused on viruses, particularly the same tobacco mosaic virus that James Watson had studied for awhile. This research was very successful, producing seventeen publications between 1953 and 1958. Tragically, her promising career was cut short by cancer, very possibly caused by the X-rays she used in her scientific work. She died on April 16, 1958, at the age of thirty-seven.

CHAPTER ELEVEN

MAPPING THE HUMAN GENOME

In 1985, a meeting was held at the University of California, Santa Cruz (UCSC) to discuss the possibility of mapping the entire human genome. This would involve mapping all 30,000 genes in human DNA, although the exact number of genes was not then known. At the time, the largest genome map that had been completed was of the Epstein-Barr virus. Although most of those at the meeting decided that this idea was infeasible, there were some who believed it could be done. One of them was Walter Gilbert, a biophysicist from Harvard University. He worked with James Watson at Harvard, and before long he had won over Watson.

The next year, another meeting was held at Los Alamos National Laboratory in New Mexico. By this time, the idea of mapping the human genome seemed more possible.

There was some concern that the $3-billion cost would take funds away from smaller projects, and some of the scientists questioned the value of the results. Despite these concerns, the project went ahead. A decision was made to map not only the human genome, but also the genomes of the mouse, the roundworm *C. elegans* and the bacteria *Escherichia coli*. Since most organisms have similar genes, a map of these other genomes could support the mapping of the human genome.

At first the Department of Energy supervised the project, but it soon moved to the National Institutes of Health (NIH). In 1988, the NIH announced the creation of the National Center for Human Genome Research (NCHGR), headed by James Watson. In 1990, the Center released a publication called "Understanding Our Genetic Inheritance: The Human Genome Project, The First Five Years." This report described a research plan for the next five years of what the NCHGR believed would be a fifteen-year project.

When Watson took over the project, there was an ongoing question about the direction it should take. Should the time and money be spent building tools like gene maps and faster sequencing machines, or should it focus on using the tools to discover genes that caused diseases?

Watson was strongly in favor of building the tools. While the disease genes caught the public's attention, he believed that in the long run it was important to do a complete sequencing, which would require better tools.[1] Others disagreed with him. J. Craig Venter, head of a large sequencing lab at the National Institute for Neurological Disorders and Stroke, was one of them. He claimed he had a new method, called expressed sequence tags, that would

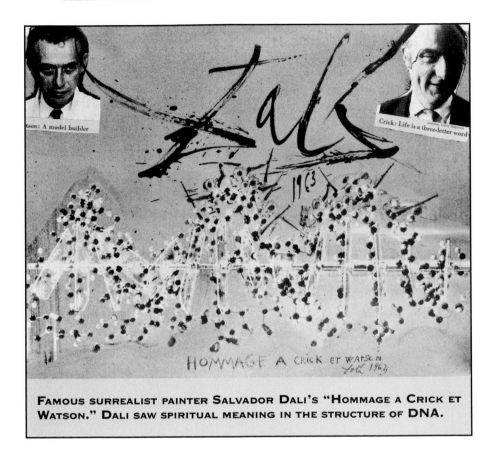

tson: A model builder

Crick: Life is a three-letter word

HOMMAGE A CRICK ET WATSON
Yoll 1963

FAMOUS SURREALIST PAINTER SALVADOR DALI'S "HOMMAGE A CRICK ET WATSON." DALI SAW SPIRITUAL MEANING IN THE STRUCTURE OF DNA.

enable him to find 80 to 90 percent of genes in a few years at a fraction of the human genome project's cost.

At a congressional hearing, Venter reported that the NIH was applying for patents on the partial genes his lab was finding at the rate of 1,000 a month. This infuriated Watson. Getting patents on the partial genes meant there was no protection for biologists who worked long and hard to identify the complete genes. His disagreement over this issue with Bernadine Healey, the head of the NIH, led to his resignation from the NCHGR in 1992. Venter also left to start his own nonprofit organization, the Institute for Genomic Research.[2]

Work on the human genome project has continued since Watson left the NCHGR. Francis S. Collins took over as director. In June 2000, the NCHGR announced that the majority of the human genome had been mapped. In February 2001, the scientific journal *Nature* published 90 percent of the genome's sequence.

James Watson continues to contribute to the world of science. In addition to his responsibilities as President of the Cold Spring Harbor Laboratory, he still writes about science. In 2002, his book, *Genes, Girls, and Gamow* was published. This was an account of what happened to him in the years following his DNA work. Like *The Double Helix*, it was a story of scientific exploration written for the non-scientist.

THE FUTURE

In the last fifty years, scientists have made great leaps forward in the ways they have applied their greater understanding of DNA to fighting diseases, solving crimes, and helping reproduction. Undoubtedly, the next fifty years will see even more amazing advances in many different fields. Many scientists have already begun speculating on what will happen in the next several decades. James Watson, for one, believes that there are still many areas for scientists to pursue:

> We've hardly skimmed off all the good stuff, so I don't feel a bit sorry for kids who are being born today. The way to do great science is to stay away from subjects that are overpopulated, and go to the frontiers. We have more frontiers now than when I was getting started. How the mind works, for example, is still a mystery. We understand the hardware, but we don't have a clue about the operating system. There are enough questions to keep people occupied for the next hundred years.[1]

Other scientists have some specific ideas. They believe that some day they will be able to grow new organs for

81

people and to cure diseases by altering their genes. People will be able to get their genomes sequenced easily and cheaply, which will allow doctors to tailor treatments for each individual. By understanding the aging process, scientists may be able to extend people's lives to well over 100 years, and help them to stay healthy and active their whole lives.[2] Other scientists are looking at DNA found in prehistoric humans and using this information to try to discover how different groups evolved from the earliest people.

In looking at all the areas that the work of Watson and Crick have opened up to us, the future looks almost limitless. Being able to map and manipulate a person's genes will likely lead to the prevention and cure of many diseases that today are incurable. Stem cell research may allow scientists to someday grow new organs and limbs for people. Cloning could allow infertile couples to have children and to help save animal and plant species that are now endangered.

In many of these areas, ethics and legislation will have to move quickly to keep up with the science. Is it right to clone humans before we understand everything about a cloned organism? Should parents use genetic engineering to produce certain desirable traits they want in their children? How will doctors decide who benefits from genetic cures to diseases? There are many questions that will need to be answered as we move into an exciting but uncertain future.

In 1962, Professor A. Engstrom concluded his presentation of the Nobel Prize to Watson, Crick, and Wilkins with words that have proven true and continue to be true as the mysteries of genetics unfold:

Today no one can really ascertain the consequences of this new exact knowledge of the mechanisms of heredity.

CRICK AND WATSON STAND ALONGSIDE A RE-CREATION OF THEIR ORIGINAL
DEMONSTRATION MODEL OF DNA.

We can foresee new possibilities to conquer disease and to gain better knowledge of the interaction of heredity and environment and a greater understanding for the mechanisms of the origin of life. In whatever direction we look we see new vistas. We can, through the discovery by Crick, Watson, and Wilkins, to quote John Kendrew, see "the first glimpses of a new world."[3]

ACTIVITIES

Explaining the structure of DNA in all its intricacies would be a complex task, but explaining its practical effects is not. In fact it is really quite easy.

Gregor Mendel, father of the field of genetics, conducted more than 20,000 experiments in an effort to understand heredity. These experiments involved crossbreeding plants with different traits. This led him to draw conclusions as to why different children of the same parents have different traits; as well as which traits were dominant and which were recessive. But before anything else, Mendel had to first make simple observations. You could learn a great deal about heredity by making some simple observations of your own.

Inherited Traits

Start with a pencil and paper. Make a list of some of your mother's physical traits, such as eye color, hair color, and height. Then make a list of your father's. Make separate lists for you and each of your siblings.

Compare the lists to see which characteristics you inherited from each parent. From which parent did you inherit most of your physical traits? Did any of your siblings also inherit the majority of their physical traits from the same parent?

Dominant or recessive?

Observe different traits in a large group of people (at least thirty). Some ideas for traits are: eye color (brown or blue), hair color (dark or light), ability to roll his or her tongue or

A MAGNIFIED VIEW OF A THUMB PRINT.

not, and whether or not the person has freckled skin. Make a table to show the traits along with how many people in the group have the different traits. Figure out the percentage of your group for each trait. Draw a conclusion as to whether you think each trait is determined by a dominant or a recessive gene.

Fingerprints

Much like one's personal DNA, an individual fingerprint is unique. As a result, fingerprinting became an important part of crime solving beginning in the 1930s. Try and observe different fingerprints to see if similar fingerprint patterns might be inherited. Gather together a sample of volunteers, some of whom are in the same families. Have each person give you a fingerprint of his or her right index finger by pressing that finger on a stamp pad and then on a piece of paper. Use a separate sheet of paper for each person. Put a number on the paper, and keep a list of which numbers belong to which person.

When you have all the fingerprints, look at them with a magnifying glass. Try to put them in categories by different patterns. Then see if family members tend to have the same fingerprints.

DNA Fingerprinting

The characteristics of any living thing can be (essentially) determined by its DNA. Much like an individual fingerprint, the DNA of each individual organism (with the exception of twins) is unique. However, while a person's fingerprint could be altered by surgery, their DNA cannot be altered. As a result, identifying someone by their DNA (known as "DNA Fingerprinting") is rapidly replacing conventional fingerprinting as a means of identification.

Crime labs across the United States use DNA finger-printing to link suspects to crimes. A drop of blood, a single hair, or even a torn article of clothing found at a crime scene can be used to identify someone with near-perfect accuracy.

As discussed previously, our understanding of DNA allows us to do much more than simply identify people. It can allow us to better treat certain illnesses, or even prevent an illness or disorder from occurring at all. None of this would be possible without the work of James Watson, Francis Crick, Maurice Wilkins, and Rosalind Franklin.

CHRONOLOGY

1916—*June 8*: Francis Crick is born in Northampton, England.
December 15: Maurice Wilkins is born in Pongaroa, New Zealand.

1920—*July 25*: Rosalind Franklin is born in London, England.

1928—*April 6*: James Watson is born in Chicago, Illinois.

1943—Watson enters the University of Chicago at age fifteen.

1947—Watson begins graduate work at the University of Indiana.

1950—Watson receives fellowship to study in Copenhagen, Denmark.

1951—*May*: Watson attends a lecture by Maurice Wilkins on X-ray crystallography of DNA.
October: Watson begins work at Cavendish Laboratory, Cambridge, England, and meets Francis Crick.
November: Watson and Crick present their first DNA model to Maurice Wilkins and Rosalind Franklin, who immediately see major problems with it.

1952—*May*: Wilkins and Franklin, unable to work out their differences, are assigned different forms of DNA to work on; Wilkins will study the B form and Franklin the A form.

1953—*January*: Linus Pauling proposes a triple helix structure for DNA; Watson sees several basic chemistry errors with Pauling's model.

February: Watson realizes that the base pairs on the DNA strand match up A–T and G–C instead of like bases pairing together.

April: Watson and Crick publish paper on DNA in the journal *Nature*.

1958—*April 16*: Rosalind Franklin dies of cancer at age thirty-seven.

1962—Watson, Crick, and Wilkins receive the Nobel Prize for Physiology or Medicine for the discovery of the structure of DNA.

1968—*March 28*: James Watson marries Elizabeth Lewis.

Watson publishes *The Double Helix*, a sometimes controversial account of his discovery of the structure of DNA. The book becomes a bestseller.

1970—A gene is created from scratch by researchers at the University of Wisconsin.

1972—The first molecules of recombinant DNA are created by Paul Berg and his colleagues via splicing genes from viruses.

1976—Watson becomes director of Cold Spring Harbor Laboratory in Long Island, New York.

Genentech, the first genetic-engineering company, is founded by Herbert Boyer and Robert Swanson.

1978—Genentech successfully clones the gene for human insulin.

1982—The first genetically engineered drug (a form of insulin) is approved by the U.S. Food and Drug Administration (FDA).

1984—Genetic fingerprinting is first developed.

1988—Watson is appointed associate director of the Human Genome Research office at the National Institutes of Health.

1989—Watson is appointed director of the Human Genome Project (a project dedicated to mapping and sequencing human DNA).
The first genetic screening test, designed to determine the gender of an embryo, is performed.
Dr. Lap-Chee Tsui discovers the gene that causes the disease cystic fibrosis.

1992—Watson resigns from the Human Genome Project and returns to Cold Spring Harbor Laboratory.

1993—A human embryo is successfully cloned at George Washington University.

1994—Watson becomes president of Cold Spring Harbor Laboratory.

1997—Ian Wilmut and his colleagues produce the first cloned sheep, which they name Dolly.

1998—Embryonic stem cells are successfully grown in a laboratory.

2000—Craig Venter and Francis Collins announce they have sequenced the human genome.

2002—Scientists at Texas A & M University successfully clone a cat, which they nickname "cc" (short for "copy cat").

2003—Royal Mint of Great Britain issues a £2 coin to commemorate the fiftieth anniversary of the discovery of the structure of DNA.

CHAPTER NOTES

Chapter 1. The Secrets of Life

1. James Watson and Francis Crick, "A Structure for Deoxyribose Nucleic Acid," *Nature*, April 25, 1953, p. 737.

2. Prof. A. Engstrom, "The Nobel Prize in Physiology or Medicine, 1962: Presentation Speech," *Nobel e-Museum*, <http://www.nobel.se/medicine/laureates/1962/press.html> (August 28, 2003).

3. James Watson, "The Involvement of RNA in the Synthesis of Proteins: Nobel Lecture, December 11, 1962," *Nobel e-Museum*, <http://www.nobel.se/medicine/laureates/1962/watson-lecture.pdf> (August 28, 2003).

Chapter 2. An Unlikely Team

1. Stephen S. Hall, "James Watson and the Search for Biology's 'Holy Grail,'" *Smithsonian*, February 1990, p. 40.

2. Paul Strathern, *Crick, Watson, and DNA* (New York: Anchor Books, 1999), pp. 47–48.

3. James D. Watson, *The Double Helix: A Personal Account of the Discovery of the Structure of DNA* (New York: Atheneum, 1968), pp. 23–24.

4. Ibid., p. 25.

5. Ibid., p. 28.

6. Ibid., pp. 31–32.

7. Strathern, pp. 50–51.

Chapter 3. A Mutual Goal

1. Francis Crick, *What Mad Pursuit: A Personal View of Scientific Discovery* (New York: Basic Books, 1988), p. 7.

2. Ibid., p. 9.

3. Paul Strathern, *Crick, Watson, and DNA* (New York: Anchor Books, 1999), p. 44.

4. Crick, pp. 17–18.

5. Strathern, p. 45.

6. James D. Watson, *The Double Helix: A Personal Account of the Discovery of the Structure of DNA* (New York: Atheneum, 1968), pp. 1, 37.

Chapter 4. Personality Clash

1. "Maurice Wilkins: DNA Enabler," *The New Zealand Edge*, n.d., <http://www.nzedge.com/heroes/wilkins.html> (August 28, 2003).

2. Francis Crick, *What Mad Pursuit: A Personal View of Scientific Discovery* (New York: Basic Books, 1988), p. 19.

3. "Maurice Wilkins," *Nobel e-Museum*, <http://www.nobel.se/medicine/laureates/1962/press.html> (August 28, 2003).

4. Crick, p. 20.

5. Anne Sayre, *Rosalind Franklin and DNA* (New York: Norton, 1975), p. 42.

6. Ibid., p. 60.

7. Ibid., p. 69.

8. Ibid., p. 85.

9. Ibid., pp. 104–106.

Chapter 5. What Is DNA?

1. Paul Strathern, *Crick, Watson, and DNA* (New York: Anchor Books, 1999), pp. 38–39.

2. Ibid., p. 40.

Chapter 6. Early Setbacks

1. Paul Strathern, *Crick, Watson, and DNA* (New York: Anchor Books, 1999), pp. 55–56.

2. Anne Sayre, *Rosalind Franklin and DNA* (New York: Norton, 1975), pp. 38–39.

3. James D. Watson, *The Double Helix: A Personal Account of the Discovery of the Structure of DNA* (New York: Atheneum, 1968), p. 37.

4. Ibid., p. 38.

5. Strathern, p. 57.

6. Watson, pp. 47–49.

7. Ibid., p. 55.

8. Sayre, pp. 133–134.

9. Watson, p. 66.

10. Strathern, p. 68.

Chapter 7. A Key Insight

1. James D. Watson, *The Double Helix: A Personal Account of the Discovery of the Structure of DNA* (New York: Atheneum, 1968), p. 76.

2. Ibid., p. 77.

3. Ibid., p. 85.

4. Paul Strathern, *Crick, Watson, and DNA* (New York: Anchor Books, 1999), pp. 71–73.

Chapter 8. The Race for DNA

1. James D. Watson, *The Double Helix: A Personal Account of the Discovery of the Structure of DNA* (New York: Atheneum, 1968), p. 99.

2. Ibid., p. 102.

3. Michael D. Lemonick, "The Secret of Life," *Time*, February 17, 2003, p. 54.

4. Watson, p. 107.

5. Ibid., p. 108.

6. Ibid.

Chapter 9. The Structure of DNA

1. Watson, James D. *The Double Helix: A Personal Account of the Discovery of the Structure of DNA* (New York: Atheneum, 1968), p. 109.

2. Paul Strathern, *Crick, Watson, and DNA* (New York: Anchor Books, 1999), pp. 86–87.

3. Watson, p. 112.

4. Ibid., p. 115.

5. Ibid., pp. 115–116.

6. Ibid., p. 116.

7. Ibid., p. 125.

8. Ibid., p. 126.

9. Ibid., p. 133.

10. Ibid., p. 138.

11. Ibid., p. 139.

12. "Fifty Year Anniversary of DNA Structure Discovery," CNN.com/ Science & Space, February 8, 2003, <http://www.cnn.com/2003/TECH/science/02/08/helix. anniversary.ap/> (December 19, 2003).

Chapter 10. Moving On

1. Michael D. Lemonick, "'You Have to Be Obsessive,'" *Time*, February 17, 2003, p. 52.

2. Brian Johnson, "James Watson," *Emuseum: Minnesota State University, Mankato*, n.d., <http:// emuseum.mnsu.edu/information/biography/uvwxyz/ watson_james.html> (August 28, 2003).

3. Paul Strathern, *Crick, Watson, and DNA* (New York: Anchor Books, 1999), pp. 86–87.

Chapter 11. Mapping the Human Genome

1. Leslie Roberts, "Controversial from the Start," *Science*, February 2001, p. 1185.

2. Ibid., p. 1186.

Chapter 12. The Future

1. Michael D. Lemonick, "You Have to Be Obsessive," *Time*, February 17, 2003, p. 52.

2. "Future Visions," *Time,* February 17, 2003, pp. 60–61.

3. "The Nobel Prize in Physiology or Medicine 1962: Presentation Speech by Professor A. Engstrom, Member of the Staff of Professors of the Royal Caroline Institute," <http://www.nobel.se/medicine/laureates/1962/press.html> (August 28, 2003).

GLOSSARY

cells—The basic unit of life. All living things are made up of cells, ranging in size from single-celled organisms to plants and animals made up of many cells. A human being has 10 trillion cells (10,000,000,000,000). Each cell has a nucleus that controls its activity.

chromosome—The structure in the cell's nucleus that contains genes. Every species has the same number of chromosomes in each of its cells. (Humans have forty-six.)

cloning—A process in which an identical organism is reproduced by injecting the nucleus of a cell from one organism into an egg cell from another. The egg cell then develops into a new plant or animal that has the exact same genes as the first organism.

crystallography—A process in which X-rays are used to study the structure of different substances. When a beam of X-rays passes through the substance, the atoms act as tiny mirrors that diffract (or spread out) the rays. A photograph can be taken of the pattern made by this diffraction. From the pattern, scientists can tell what the structure of the substance looks like.

DNA (deoxyribonucleic acid)—A substance found in the cells of almost all living things. Genes are made up of DNA. When a cell divides, the DNA provides the instructions for that cell's development.

gene—The parts of the cell that determine which characteristics a living organism inherits from its parents. Genes are located on the chromosomes, and each cell has thousands of genes. Genes are made up of deoxyribonucleic acid (DNA).

genetics—The study of heredity, or how characteristics are passed from parents to their offspring. Scientists who study genetics are called geneticists. They study how genes work.

genome—The location of genes on a chromosome, which can be represented as a "map."

helix—A spiral form or structure.

molecule—The smallest unit of matter that still contains the same properties as that matter. For instance, a molecule of water is the smallest amount of water that is still water. If divided further, it breaks down into its base components of hydrogen and oxygen atoms.

protein—Large molecules made up of smaller units called amino acids. Proteins exist in every cell of living things.

FURTHER READING

Allan, Tony. *Understanding DNA*. Chicago: Heinemann Library, 2002.

Bankston, John. *Francis Crick and James Watson: Pioneers in DNA Research*. Bear, Del.: Mitchell Lane Publishers, 2002.

Boon, Kevin Alexander. *The Human Genome Project*. Berkeley Heights, N.J.: Enslow Publishers, Inc., 2002.

Edelson, Edward. *Francis Crick and James Watson: And the Building Blocks of Life*. New York: Oxford University Press, Inc., 2000.

Newton, David E. *James Watson & Francis Crick: Discovery of the Double Helix and Beyond*. New York: Facts on File, 1992.

Pasachoff, Naomi. *Linus Pauling: Advancing Science, Advocating Peace*. Berkeley Heights, N.J.: Enslow Publishers, Inc., 2004.

Sherrow, Victoria. *James Watson & Francis Crick: Decoding the Secrets of DNA*. Farmington Hills, Mich.: Gale Group, 1995.

Silverstein, Alvin, et al. *DNA*. Brookfield, Conn.: Millbrook Press, Inc., 2002.

INTERNET ADDRESSES

Biographical Sketch of James Dewey Watson
http://www.cshl.org/public/SCIENCE/Watson.html

Create A DNA Fingerprint
http://www.pbs.org/wgbh/nova/sheppard/analyze.html

Genetic Science Learning Center at the Eccles Institute of Human Genetics
http://gslc.genetics.utah.edu/

The Human Genome Project
http://www.ncbi.nlm.nih.gov/genome/guide/human

Nobel e-Museum
http://www.nobel.se/

INDEX